Confronting Holocaust Denial

Deslee Campbell

In memory of my dear friend and Holocaust survivor,
musicologist Ida Ferson, of blessed memory,
who worked to keep
the memory of the Shoah
and the music of Theresienstadt
alive.

Bible quotations are from the Interlinear Bible translation with Hebrew text. Trinitarian Bible Society London, © 1976.

DESLEE CAMPBELL

Table of Contents

"So I returned and considered all the oppressions that are done under the sun. And behold the tears of those who were oppressed and they had no comforter! And at the hand of those who oppressed them was power, but there was no comforter to them.

Therefore I commended the dead who already have died, more than the living who are alive unto now."

Ecclesiastes 4:1-2

Prologue

During the Hitler Years (1933-1945) many thousands of ordinary European people saw and knew quite a lot about one or other aspect of the planned genocide, which Hitler was perpetrating upon the Jewish people; but they diverted their faces so that they would not see the obvious, or turned their backs so that they would not have to help.

Today, still, most people just don't want to know; it is all too horrible to bear thinking about. These days, when, once again, lies and ignorance walk hand in hand across the earth, good people must equip themselves with knowledge, to which, perhaps, this little book will contribute. After all, evil men only flourish when good men do nothing.

In these days of the resurgence of Nazi ideology we must confront the issues. Our response to it must be active and assertive - without being aggressive. It must be positive and pro-active, not reactive, defensive, passive or hesitant. An active educational campaign and study of the facts and issues is the best way to withstand the propaganda onslaught of those in the world community who deny the Holocaust.

The subject is so monumental and of such powerful significance that it warrants our best efforts. This striving for understanding must therefore be thorough, truthful and rigorous; and we must remember that there is hardly a nation on earth not enmeshed in the Holocaust to a greater or lesser degree. It is not just Jewish business; it is our business.

We must however, remember that while the Holocaust is world history it is also primarily the Holocaust of the Jewish people of Europe. We must not universalise its message to the extent that we generalise their suffering and marginalise their threatened genocide.

There are a number of key aspects to denial. Some deniers claim that the whole story of the Holocaust is a fake, invented to justify the founding of the State of Israel, by the United Nations in 1948. Others devalue its magnitude, claiming that the conventional wisdom on the subject is exaggerated in size and scope. Members of this second group call themselves 'History Revisionists', rather than 'Holocaust Deniers'. But in both cases lies must be counted with truth and ignorance with facts, disseminated through education.

The confrontational aspects of Holocaust denial, which are an outrage to our sensibilities and deeply offensive to our human feelings, operate not in the intellect but in the areas of the emotions. They pose an insidious attack upon our souls. An adequate means of countering this attack must therefore include not only historical fact but insights into the motivations and aims of the denier.

Holocaust denial and those lies which masquerade under the euphemistic title 'Revisionist History' currently pose one of the greatest threats to truth and to the Jewish people in the world today. Under a pseudo-academic cloak the magnitude of Jewish suffering in this history is belittled and the Jewish people are labelled with the old stereotype of greedy materialists who acquire ill gotten gains by fraudulent means. The Jewish people in general, and Israel in particular, are accused of exaggeration, even of inventing lies, in order to squeeze 'conscience money' out of Germany, in the form of reparations. This accusation lies at the very centre of Holocaust denial.

By virulent attacks upon the historical truth of Nazi genocide, the legitimacy of the founding of the State of Israel in 1948, and therefore its ongoing existence, is attacked. This is based upon the rationale that without the deeds committed in the gas chambers of the death camps, the State of Israel would never have existed; and that Israel has no other justification, certainly, in their opinion, neither a Biblical nor a humanitarian justification. This is an hypothesis which Israel has always staunchly rejected.

Another euphemism must be mentioned: that of anti-Zionism. Since the victory of liberal democracy in the West it has not been politically credible to be anti-Jewish, nor anti-Judaism. That would be blatantly intolerant, racist. But to be 'anti-Zionist' appears to be politically acceptable, and increasing in acceptance, given the strength of the pro-Palestinian lobby in the world media. Yet in the Holocaust denier's use of the word 'Zionist' it is synonymous with 'Jewish'. This is a deliberate smokescreen of semantics and logic. We must avoid being confused by it.

To recapitulate: In order to adequately confront Holocaust denial we require first an insight into the methods and strategies which they use, secondly an adequate grasp of the facts and thirdly an understanding of the key and pivotal issues on which their revision of history rests.

Apart from slanders against Jews and the delegitimisation of Israel, which these slanders are supposed to substantiate, there are two other key issues. The first is the claim that no plan to slaughter the Jews ever existed and secondly the equally false idea that if such a plan did exist it was hatched by Himmler and Heydrich and kept secret from Hitler. This notion enables Hitler's reputation as a great leader to be unsullied and Nazi ideology, **his** ideology, to be embraced with a clear conscience. Clear documentary evidence does exist to show that both of these claims are false.

It should not surprise us that Holocaust denial exists because denial was built in to the system from the very beginning by virtue of the attempted concealment of all traces of the Nazi's most dastardly deeds and the elimination of all eye-witnesses to those deeds.

Prisoners were forced to send postcards to relatives assuring them of their safety 'in the east' and every effort was made to conceal from people the fate which awaited them. As one witness at the Nuremberg Trials said: *"in June and July 1944, an orchestra made up of prisoners, girls in white blouses and dark blue skirts, all of them pretty and young, who played gay tunes when the trains arrived, "The Merry Widow" and the Barcarolle from the "Tales From Hoffmann,"etc. They were told it was a labour camp..... They could not know what awaited them."*[1]

As the decades go by and the war time generation of eye witnesses and survivors passes the revisionists form ever stronger links with anti-Semitic political groupings like Neo-Nazis, Fascists, Ultra-nationalists, anarchists, Skin Heads, Pamyat in the former Soviet Union and Palestinian terrorist organisations. This will inevitably result in an increase in the negative effects of militant Holocaust denial and the sponsoring of anti-Semitic attitudes and actions. Positive and informed counter measures are necessary to prevent pseudo-academic Jew hatred, especially amongst young intellectuals. Students are the group most targeted by the deniers; as one of their number said: "*I don't want to spend time with adults any more. I want to go to students. They are superficial. They are empty vessels to be filled.*"

So effective has the push for publicity by the party of Holocaust deniers become, that the debate has not been contained in the halls of academia but is out on the streets, on television screens and on the front pages of our leading newspapers. the older generation remembers enough real information, and the emotional impact which the revealing of those facts generated, to be cynical of their efforts, but the youth, who are targeted across the globe, are perplexed, confused or even intrigued.

Neo-Nazism and Far-Right extremism is on the rise again in Europe so this matter is now current affairs, probably more so than past history.

Chapter 1
Strategies Used

Holocaust deniers use a mixture of strategies in order to maximise falsehood and minimise truth.

1) They begin by sowing doubt in the mind of the individual, doubt about a minor detail or two. This undermines the foundations of conviction.

2) Their techniques include placing the onus of proof on <u>you</u>, the average person. You are challenged to prove (as if in a court of law) that a generally accepted aspect of the Holocaust is factual. This is to say that the deniers do no accept the responsibility to prove that it is false. To the layman such a challenge is very disquieting.

3) They misquote, distort, quote out of context and even falsify the writing of recognised experts: even Jewish experts.

4) They quote spurious scientific data and falsely claim to be experts in technical and scientific fields.

5) They misuse emotionally loaded terminology.

6) They elicit our sympathy by claiming to be persecuted and misunderstood.

7) They cleverly whitewash the guilty, especially Hitler.

8) They accuse the innocent, the very victims themselves, of guilt.

9) They are academically dishonest because they ignore enormous amounts of hard evidence: good documentary evidence and court evidence.

10) Some falsify their academic credentials, achievements and/or employment history to claim or overstate their expertise.

There are many examples of the above nine points: Here are but a few.

1) Doubt about a detail: such as the arguments about whether there were gas chambers in Dachau. By throwing doubt on this matter Holocaust deniers hope that such doubt would generalise from Dachau to Auschwitz and other camps.

2) Challenge of Proof: They challenge the ordinary person to prove that Hitler knew about the killings. This issue has required in-depth technical study over many years and the general public is not in a position to know of the findings; but as total dictator Hitler held total moral responsibility for his regime. His dictatorial power was unquestioned. "The buck stopped with Hitler." Besides this Hitler's knowledge or lack of knowledge does not alter the statistics or the nature of the deeds done.

3) Misquotations: They misquote and misuse the words of Jewish historians; for example Yehuda Bauer, Raoul Hilberg and Yaacov Lozowic, world experts and/or staff members of Yad Vashem's World Centre for the Study of the Holocaust. By misusing or misquoting a few isolated phrases of these and other recognised Jewish experts they try to give legitimacy and respectability to their claims.

4) Spurious expertise: Fred Leuchter claimed to be an engineer dealing but it was proven in a Boston court that he was not an engineer, but he has a Bachelor of Arts in history.

Leuchter claimed to have made

This was declared to be fake evidence, inadmissible in court; though 'The Leuchter Reports' are still acclaimed by Holocaust deniers as proof that the Auschwitz saga is a lie.

5) Emotive terms: Terms such as "Myth of the Six Million", "Hoax of the Six Million", "Holohoax" are used to slander the Holocaust traditionalists, and therefore the victims.

6) Extraction of sympathy: Holocaust deniers claim to be, not the supporters of discrimination and persecution, but its victims. For example: "(We) have been subject to smear campaigns, loss of academic

positions, loss of pensions, destruction of property and physical violence".

7) Whitewash of the guilty: They claim that Hitler did not know of the mass extermination of the Jews, refusing to review recent evidence to the contrary and ignoring Hitler's moral and legal responsibility as sole dictator. One Holocaust Denier, Austin App, claimed that the majority of Jews who died were in Soviet controlled territory, not German controlled territory. This, of course, whitewashes the Germans, while making the Stalinist Russians to be even blacker than they deserve to be.

8) Accusing the victims of guilt: They say, for example, that the Jews of the world "declared war on Germany". They have invented a preposterous defamation, accusing the Zionists of collaboration with the Nazis (presumably to force the Jews to flee to Palestine and so to populate it).

In actual fact it was the infamous Muslim Grand Mufti of Jerusalem, Haj Amin al Husseini, who collaborated with the Nazis. He was personally received by Hitler on 28/11/'41, given a personal tour of a concentration camp by the Fuhrer and spent 2½ years in Germany assisting the Axis war effort. In Croatia the Mufti personally raised `Handjar'(Sword), a Moslem battalion of 20,000 men. They massacred civilians and fought partisans in Bosnia with the Waffen SS; hunted Jews in Croatia; and did police and security duty in Hungary. The Fuhrer assured Husseini that, once victorious, he would *promise the annihilation of the Jews living under British protection in Arab lands*".[2]

9) Academic dishonesty: The deniers shift disproportionate blame onto the Allies. They accuse the Allies of killing more people in bombing raids than the number who died in the concentration camps. They accuse the Soviets, Americans and British of torturing German prisoners to extract confessions for use in the Nuremberg trials. As though two wrongs make one right they accuse the British of themselves setting up the first concentrations camps, during the Boer War, which one Holocaust denier has claimed were *"far worse that any concentration camp*

of World War II". While these camps did exist it is a gross exaggeration to say that they were "*Hell holes in which tens of thousands (of Dutch women and children) died*". In fact between 1900 and 1901 in 44 camps, 6000 white adults and 1000 children died; mainly of measles and dysentery.

Plate 1. The Famous Entrance Gate to Auschwitz I.
Photo: David Campbell, 1992.

Chapter 2
Who are the Deniers?

It is important to know that although they have been few in number, Holocaust deniers seek a high profile. In the 20th century they formed a world-wide set, reinforcing each other, quoting each other, publicising each other and using the same few publishing houses. Some are still active in the field but they have been overtaken since the Covid pandemic by more violent anti-Semitism and anti-Zionism on the streets and university campuses of the Western World.

History Revisionism

DAVID IRVING

David Irving is the best known 'History revisionist' but real deniers disassociate themselves from him because he admits that there were deliberate murders, which they generally deny. He is regarded as too moderate; his view is 'soft revisionism'. An example of this would be the opinion that the killings were carried out by non-German members of killing squads (under SS control), but never in gas chambers. This is a half-truth: the first half of it is true.

Australia was racked by a controversy when David Irving made many numerous attempts to enter the country to lecture. He was denied because Neo-Nazis always turned out to support him, which caused security concerns for the police and because it would be contrary to social cohesion in a multi-racial society. Irving's views are expounded in his substantial work *"Hitler's War"* which proposes that Hitler had no knowledge of the "final solution". There is a subtle attempt to rehabilitate Hitler as *"a man of enormous sensitivity and charm, a man of courage and principle, despite the corruption and rivalry of his entourage"*.[3] Irving is the only major revisionist to have had formal training in history and his writing is closely researched. History revisionism is in a separate class from Holocaust denial.

Holocaust Denial

HARRY BARNES

American, Harry Barnes died in 1968. It was he who coined the term "historical blackout". This term suggests that publishers attempted to gag certain points of view by refusing to publish their work. This term passed into general use and later came to mean the work of "the Thought Police" that is, anyone who disagreed with what the deniers were claiming.

PAUL RASSINIER

This French writer and teacher died in 1967. He was a former Buchenwald political prisoner, deported for resistance activities, who had obviously seen few atrocities. A French court found his writings to be Fascist. His main works were *"Debunking the Genocide Myth"*, and *"The Real Eichmann Trials"*.

THIES CHRISTOPHERSON

Christopherson, a German, was a one-time Wehrmacht officer and a guard in the Raisko Camp. This was a part of the Auschwitz complex in which slave labourers were housed. As such it was not part of the extermination machinery. He wrote *"The Auschwitz Lie"*, which painted an idolised picture of life in Auschwitz. He died in 1997.

ROBERT FAURISSON

Faurisson died in 2018. He was Associate Professor of French literature at the University of Lyon but was suspended from his position. In 1981 a French court found him guilty of: 1) slander, 2) inciting racial hatred, 3) wilfully distorting history.

AUSTIN APP

American Austin App was a professor of English who was a Nazi sympathiser as early as the 1940s and who denied that extermination had any place in Nazi ideology. He claimed that Russia was responsible for most of the Jewish deaths and that the figure of six million is grossly exaggerated. He wrote many pamphlets; plus *"The Six Million Swindle."* He died in 1984.

ARTHUR BUTZ

Dr Butz, an American professor of engineering, wrote *"The Hoax of the 20th Century"* (1976) and "The Fabrication of a Hoax" (1977).

FRED LEUCHTER

Fred Leuchter was born in 1943 and wrote his *First Leuchter Report* in 1988 about his secret, scientific study of samples he took from the gas chambers of Auschwitz. It was declared inadmissible as science, in court. His *Second Leuchter Report* was written in 1989/1990. In 1999, Errol Morris made a documentary about Leuchter's life called "Mr Death. The Rise and Fall of Fred A. Leuchter, Jr". For a transcript see: ErrolMorris.com

Apart from David Irving, none of the above had training in history. Most had qualifications in literature, which was of obvious assistance when writing their books.

The *"Protocols of the Elders of Zion"*.

`The Protocols', is an obvious influence. It has been reprinted by the thousands in at least 21 different countries in 42 post-war editions, in many languages (including Arabic). It purports to be Jewish but is a complete fabrication.

Plate 2. Remembering the Six Million.
Photo: Deslee Campbell, 1990.

What Are Their Motives?

The motives of the groups and individuals noted appear to be varied. Germans, or old style Nazis from the war years, wanted to white-wash their past, or white-wash their glorious national leader, Hitler, who would, like a good father, have prevented the killings if he had known of them. This accompanies the claim that Chaim Weizmann declared war on Germany on behalf of World Jewry, in 1939, as a result of which

Himmler and Heydrich eventually developed the policy of internment, in which Hitler was not involved.

In some writers, strong Jew hatred, self-aggrandisement and excessive anger are discernible. Envy of perceived Jewish prosperity is strongly influenced by the "*Jewish world economic conspiracy theory*" which is widely promulgated by "The Protocols of the Elders of Zion".

There is also evidence of the philosophy of racial superiority, which is not exclusive to Hitler or the Nazis.

Dislike of the creation of a Jewish State has led some to propose that the Holocaust is a gigantic lie created by Zionist propaganda to make people support Israel; or to extract reparations from Germany, or both.

German Responses

In the late 1970s a controversy in Victoria, Australia, surrounded a lawyer (who was dismissed from employment for distributing the writings of well-known Holocaust deniers). The West German embassy responded by mounting an exhibition, with the help of the Jewish community, to affirm that indeed the Third Reich had undertaken to destroy all the Jews of Europe.

The German government has always accepted the traditional facts. Usually reparations and pension payments are willingly made to survivors and families. With the unification of East and West Germany, payments were voluntarily extended to eligible Jews who once lived in former East Germany. One of the first acts of the United German Parliament was to stand in silence in a tribute to the victims of the Holocaust. Even now the German government does not engage in Holocaust denial and is very supportive of Israel.

Chapter 3
Tactics and Weapons

The hidden weapon of Holocaust deniers, in their battle for the minds of the next generation, is to foster the assumption that our knowledge of the Holocaust rests on very little evidence and flimsy evidence at that. If they can confuse people and sow doubt about a few facts, they can undermine confidence in the entire fabric.

The truth is that this epoch is the most thoroughly documented and validated period of world history; bar none. During the entire course of civilised history no other event has been so thoroughly scrutinised, scientifically researched, and argued in courts of law than World War II, of which the Holocaust is a key component. The period was extensively documented by all protagonists during the conflict and documents from both Allied and Axis sources confirm each other. Testimony from both victims and perpetrators has been meticulously collected for eight decades and some of the best legal and academic minds, in both the West and the communist worlds, have been dedicated to extracting and evaluating the truth.

No one doubts the facts of Captain Cook's journey to Botany Bay or Julius Caesar's campaigns in Gaul, but the hard evidence that we have in proof of these is infinitesimal compared with the vast mass of written, photographic, oral and forensic evidence which is readily available on the period called the Shoah. Enormous quantities of documentary material, as yet not analysed has been released from Soviet archives since the democratic revolution in the USSR. From c.1990, at last, the remaining eye witnesses and survivors who were previously afraid to testify are free to speak.

The task of collating, translating, analysing and evaluating this vast mass of new evidence is enormous. Perhaps this data will require some re-writing of accepted Holocaust history, but the Jewish people are not afraid to seek the truth. This data is currently leading the experts to believe that the estimate of victims, now standing at six million, will be exceeded by the time the Soviet material has all been analysed. Certainly the deniers figure of fewer that half a million victims is ludicrous.

Holocaust deniers try to make people believe that the Holocaust rests on a foundation of only a few pieces of evidence. By successfully challenging one of those foundational pieces of evidence, the structure will collapse. The truth is, however, that the Shoah does not rest upon a few pieces of evidence, not even on a few <u>categories</u> of evidence, but upon a vast multitude of individual pieces of available evidence, which fall into many categories. Each category contains more than sufficient evidence to rest a legal case upon, yet deniers attack minute parts and hope that the vast mass of similar or superior evidence will be overlooked. By this they hope to convince us that the case has broken down and the day lost. Consider, for example, the focus upon the question of the small gas-chamber of Dachau, this is concentrated upon in order to deflect attention from the real issue: the gas chambers of Auschwitz-Birkenau.

Take also the example of the continual attacks on the authenticity of *"The Diary of Anne Frank."* The deniers hope that by throwing doubt on such a well-known example, such a highly respected symbol, the confidence of young people in the whole Holocaust fabric will be threatened. By attacking a major symbol of Jewish heroism under persecution they can undermine the whole saga.

Mr Otto Frank successfully sued David Irving for his claim that the Diary was a forgery. Irving withdrew the claim, but deniers continue to claim that it is a fake, despite the forensic examinations undertaken by the Dutch Government to settle the matter once and for all.

Was Anne Frank's the only diary? Of course not; it wasn't even the only teenager's diary. Many adults and other young people, who were not as isolated, who saw and knew much more, wrote in more detail and the contents of their writings were more inditing. Take, for example, the words of a teenage slave-labourer, Berek Sitenfeld, pencilled as he faced the final liquidation of the Chelmno Death Camp in Poland: "*When the war began I was eleven. During the five years in the Ghetto I suffered a lot, and there was nothing I could do to help my dear parents. How painful it is to watch one's father dying of hunger, without any possibility of helping him. Just imagine my experiences! Now, when I see how many innocent Jews and Poles perish in such a dreadful manner, my heart aches and I desire to avenge all of them. But here is a sixteen year old boy shackled like a bandit, surrounded on all sides by barrels of machine guns..... Let my family know about me, this is my last request before I die*".[4]

Nothing in Anne Frank's interesting writings has the power, immediacy and anguish of these words, yet these are just <u>one</u> example of the heart-rending thoughts of <u>one</u> young victim in his last hours. Shoah History, as it relates to youth, does not rest, irrevocably, upon Anne Frank, but because she has become a world-wide symbol of children of the Holocaust, her work remains in the firing line. This author's book "Voices From the Silence" analysis the diaries of four teenagers who perished in the Shoah, one of whom was Anne Frank. It is available as an ebook from many outlets.

Chapter 4
The Final Solution

The term 'Final Solution' is the somewhat euphemistic title for the master plan of genocide against the Jews: Hitler's plan to annihilate all the Jews of Europe (as a first step). It was a plan which succeeded in eliminating two thirds of them, approximately 6,000,000 people, that is one in every five Jews in the entire world.

PLANS FOR THE FINAL SOLUTION

Even Holocaust revisionists, like David Irving, admit the concentration camps were 'Slave Labour camps' and that multitudes died of starvation and disease in them. They deny, however, that these deaths were intentional, and not simply the natural consequences of epidemics transmitted by lice. Yet these deaths were <u>not</u> purely accidental. They were part of an overall plan.

Had the Third Reich endured for the thousand years that Hitler planned, he would have extended his genocidal machinery wherever his rule expanded beyond Europe. Hitler had already discussed his plans for the treatment of Jews in Palestine, Lebanon and Turkey, and had well formulated intentions with regard to the Jews of neutral nations such as Spain, Turkey, Sweden and Switzerland. These Jews appear on the detailed inventory of potential victims drawn up in 1941: 6,000 from Spain, 55,500 from Turkey 8,000 from Sweden, 18,000 from Switzerland, and so on. The Jews of Ireland (40,00) and of Britain (330,000) were also demarcated for future slaughter. Even the 200 Jews of Albania were not overlooked in the planning for the Final Solution.[5]

During a conference held in the Berlin suburb of Wannsee, on the 20th January 1942, now known as the *Wannsee Conference*, the principles of the 'Final Solution' became policy and thereafter the term

'Immanent Final Solution' came to replace the previously used terminology.

Clear documentary evidence has been unearthed to prove that there was a clear and spoken intention to rid Europe of its entire Jewish population, by expulsion, by working them to death and by murdering them.

The official, and heavily edited minutes of the Wannsee Conference (20/1/42), for example, read: *"Jews capable of work will be moved into these areas as they build roads during which a large proportion will no doubt drop out through natural reduction. The remnant which eventually remains will require suitable treatment....(because it) could, on its release, become the germ cell of a new Jewish revival".*[6]

This short paragraph clearly reveals the deliberate policy of working the Jews to death and hints at more secret and more unmentionable treatment.

How horrendous that a civilised, Christian, Western nation should have kept slaves whom they starved and deliberately worked to death. This admission alone, even without a policy of murder, is an indictment of Nazi policy and behaviour.

The Wannsee Conference defined a Jew by invoking the September, 1935, Nuremberg Laws of Reich Citizenship, and of German Blood and German Honour. By the Laws pertaining to Second Degree Mixed-blood, people of Jewish appearance, alone, or behaving or feeling like a Jew, classed the person as Jewish. Some people of 'mixed blood', like some disabled people, could undergo 'voluntary' sterilisation to avoid deportation and death.

Unofficially extermination was discussed at the Wannsee Conference, but the extermination program was, in fact, already under-way: the Chelmno death camp had already been operating for a month, <u>and</u> construction of Belzec had already started.

The purpose of the Wannsee Conference was to gain a consensus, to spread guilt to a wider group beyond the inner circle of Hitler, Goring,

Himmler and Heydrich; and to secure power for Heydrich, who over-saw the conference. It was also designed to gain the cooperation of, and therefore to implicate, the four Secretaries of State in the Reich (Stuckart, Neumann, Freisler and Buhler).

Heydrich invoked *"previous approval through the Fuhrer"* while his November invitations, sent to potential delegates, included an authorisation which Goring, Hitler's Prime Minister, had signed on July 31, 1942. The 'Final Solution' was being hatched behind the scenes for quite a long time: but from the Wannsee meeting onwards it was official.

Even when it was patently obvious that Germany was losing the war, resources were diverted from the war effort to the primary purpose of extermination, and to the concealment of the grizzly evidence. Thousands upon thousands of buried bodies were exhumed for mass cremation. At Babi-Yar the perhaps 100,000 bodies of the Jews of Kiev, who had been gunned down at the tops of the ravines in just three days: 28-30th September 1941; were exhumed by Jewish Sonder-Kommandos, who broke out in a rebellion shortly before their grizzly task was complete. They had no other choice: all eye-witnesses knew that they would be shot.

Similarly all traces of the death camps of Treblinka and Sobibor were obliterated; there was an uprising at Treblinka on 7th August '43; and a similar eleventh hour uprising at Sobibor on 14th October, 1943[7], survived by only nineteen people.

An examination of Hitler's ideological position even before the war began, provides evidence of a reasonably well- formulated plan to liquidate the Jews.

1) Hitler's ideological position before his rise to power.

As early as 1920 Nazi Party policy included this: *"The East European Jews in Germany must be got rid of without delay and ruthless measures taken against all other Jews."*

On April 29, 1920 he said: *"We will carry on the struggle until the last Jew is removed from the German Reich."*

In 1922 Hitler wrote in an essay about *"the Jewish dictatorship of Blood and its satanic infamy* (in Soviet Russia)."

In 1928 in *"Hitler's Secret Book"* he wrote: *"here* (in Germany) *it is the Nazi movement alone which has taken upon itself the struggle against this excreable crime against mankind"*.

In 1925 in *"Mein Kamph"* Hitler wrote of the Jew: *"He stops at nothing in his vileness, he becomes so gigantic that no one needs be surprised if among our people the personification of the devil as the symbol of all evil assumes the living shape of the Jew"* and *"Had we put under poison gas, before World War I or in its course, 12,000 or 15,000 or more of those Hebrew corrupters, we would have saved a million German lives so dear for the future."*

2) **Information from Hitler's speeches as Fuhrer.**

At the Kroll Opera House on the 30th January 1939 Hitler enunciated some of his key obsessions:

_ Living space for the Germans

_ Racial purity

_Jewish/ Bolshevik plot

_Jewish international financial plot.

He said: *"sooner or later* (Jews) *will succumb to a crisis of inconceivable magnitude"* and also spoke of *"the destruction of the Jewish race in Europe"*.

3) **Information given by inner circle about Fuhrer's wishes**

Here are a few examples:

_Immediately following Kristallnacht (two nights of orchestrated pogroms against Jewish shops, homes and synagogues) on the 12th November 1938, Goring told the Air Ministry: *"I have received a letter on the Fuhrer's orders from Head of Staff Bormann, with instructions that the Jewish Question be summed up and coordinated once and for all and solved one way or another. A phone call from the Fuhrer to me yesterday again gave me instructions that decisive coordinated steps must now be outlined."*[8]

_ On the 16th December 1941, Frank, the governor General of Occupied Eastern Europe, said: *"One way or another - I will tell you quite openly we must finish off the Jews. The Fuhrer put it into words once... we must destroy the Jews wherever we find them... The Jew are also exceptionally harmful, we have perhaps 3½ million altogether with persons who have Jewish kin.... We cannot shoot these 3½ million, we cannot poison them, but we will be able to take measures that will lead somehow to successful destruction."*[9]

4) **Evidence and records from other Nazis.**

_ In August 1942 an engineer's notes record his discussion with the Commander of `Operation Reinhard': *"S.S.Gruppenfuhrer Globocnik said; 'this is one of the most highly secret matters there are, perhaps the most secret. Any one who speaks about it is shot immediately'. He then described the death camps Belzec, Treblinka and Sobibor (which he never saw), Majdanek, which he only saw being built. Globocnik reported to the engineer that Hitler and Himmler had been there the day before and ordered that no one see the installations unless accompanied by Globocnik. When asked what the Fuhrer said, Globocnik replied 'The whole aktion must be carried out much faster'. When Globocnik said they should bury bronze plaques with the bodies inscribed that it was we who had the courage to complete this gigantic task' Hitler complimented him saying 'Well my good Globocnik, you have said it and that is my opinion too'".*[10]

_ In October 1942, a youth leader of the Vilna Ghetto urged ghetto leaders that they must fight so that Nazi ideologist Rosenberg's words would not come true. He told them that Rosenberg, Foreign Minister and Minister for Occupied Eastern Territories, had said: *"It is the task of the Germans to exterminate the Jewish people in Europe".*[11]

While a background attitude of anti-Semitism, or unadulterated Jew-hatred, must have existed throughout Europe it is clear from the above evidence that Hitler's ideology was the most powerful force both permitting and driving the multitude of individual murderous acts by which the millions of Jewish victims died. We must therefore look in detail into the question "What did Hitler really know about the `Nazi killing machine'"?

Chapter 5
What Hitler Knew

It is not surprising that doubt has been thrown on Hitler's part in the Holocaust tragedy, as he deliberately kept a distance between himself and the events, as well as the orders for those events, especially early in the war. This, and the Nazi's determination to keep secret their most brutal deeds, has aided the cause of Holocaust denial.

Wherever possible Hitler used a chain of verbal commands, and verbal briefings; reluctant to commit anything to writing. Hitler walked with Himmler out-of-doors, while giving his orders, so that no one would overhear them.

Hitler also ordered, on 11th July 1943, that no public mention should ever be made of "*a future overall solution*" to the Jewish question, but only to "*appropriate labour purposes*"[12]

Earlier, in 1942, SS men who took part in the mass shootings in Poland, an *Aktion* code-named 'Operation Reinhard', had to sign a six point obligation to observe secrecy, "*even after I have left the service.*"[13]

Both Adolf Eichmann (SS Obersturmbannfuhrer Gestapo Head of Jewish Affairs) and Rudolf Hoss (Commander of Auschwitz) testified that Heinrich Himmler (Reichsfuhrer SS. Chief of Police and Minister of the Interior) and Reinhard Heydrich (SS Obergruppenfuhrer. Head of Reich Security Main Office) had passed on Fuhrer's Orders to them.

At his trial in 1961 Eichmann said that everyone at the Wannsee Conference had spoken openly about extermination and that everyone knew of the activities of the shooting squads (the Einsatzgruppen). By that date these squads had succeeded in rendering Estonia entirely "Jew free."

In his autobiography Rudolf Hoss wrote that Himmler told him that Hitler had ordered the Jewish question to be solved once and for all and that we, the SS, had to implement the order.[14] In his sworn testimony Hoss said: "*Himmler said in effect - 'The Fuhrer has ordered that the Jewish question be solved once and for all, and that we, the SS, are to implement that order. The existing extermination centres in the East are not in a position to carry out the large Aktionen which are anticipated. I have therefore earmarked Auschwitz for this purpose... You will treat this matter as absolutely secret, even from your superiors... The Jews are the sworn enemies of the German people and must be eradicated. Every Jew that we can lay our hands on is to be destroyed during the war, without exception.'*"[15]

Reich Kommisar Erich Koch, at his trial, said: "*I received the orders to liquidate directly from Hitler.*" Back in 1942 Koch had told a Polish doctor: "*we have shot all the Jews. It was Hitler's Order.*"

One typewriter is of particular significance. This typewriter was one of a kind. It was constructed especially for Hitler, with especially large characters, and was called the 'Fuhrer Typewriter.' Only documents for Hitler's viewing were typed on it. As many of these documents have been preserved we can know what was intended for Hitler's gaze. Some of these documents have the signed initials of those who dispatched them still clearly visible, and they record which men were to receive one of the very few copies made.

Here is one example: on 1st April, 1943 an abridged form of Korerr's statistical examination of the Final Solution (but eliminating the term 'special treatment') was typed on this typewriter. It was eventually returned from Himmler to Eichmann marked "*The Fuhrer has taken note - destroy. H.H.*"

The German propensity for orderly bureaucracy, if not Eichmann's obedience to orders, has proven to be Hitler's undoing.

Two very revealing series of events, which took place in the dying days of the Third Reich, illustrate Hitler's attitude. Germany was in great need of war materials. Himmler contacted Jewish leaders abroad, through Swiss go-betweens, which led to the surrender to the Swiss of 1200 Jewish prisoners, in exchange for trucks and war materials. Himmler's actions were opposed by Eichmann and Buhler and Klatenbrunner, who reported the deal to Hitler on 6/2/45. Hitler made a violent scene and accused Himmler of betraying him.

Himmler attempted to stop the killings at Mauthausen and Ravensbruck, possibly to enhance his chances in the face of an imminent Allied victory. The camp commandants, however, refused to obey Himmler, saying that they had "*explicit Fuhrer Orders to liquidate them*" (i.e.,the remaining prisoners). [Fortunately, when Ravensbruck was liberated on 29th April, 1945, 3,500 sick women were still alive.]

It is certain that Hitler brought great pressure to bear on the Regent of Hungary, Admiral Horthy, to surrender the Jews of Hungary for deportation, in June and July of 1944; something that Horthy had displayed great reluctance to do.

Propaganda Minister Goebbel's Diary entry of 27/3/'42 makes macabre reading: "*It is a pretty barbarous business, and it is best not to mention details but the Fuhrer's threat of annihilation was to be realised in the most dreadful manner. We must not be sentimental in these matters. It is war to the death between the Aryan race and the Jewish bacillus. Here too the Fuhrer is the inflexible champion of a radical solution.*"

Hitler deliberately encouraged a policy of maximum ambiguity, secrecy and concealment[16]. Denial was built into his plans. Yet his hatred for the Jews was expressed even in his last testament, written the day of his suicide. His accusation that World Jewry had given birth to communism, and was bent on world domination and economic take-over, owes its origins to the *"Protocols of the Elders of Zion"*, and was his unending and obsessive pre-occupation, up to his last hours.

There is no way that the mass killings were mere accidental deaths; and there is no way that Hitler's hand was not firmly in control. His philosophies and his orders motivated or directed the actions of all true German Nazis.

Chapter 6
The Shooting Squads

The *Aktinen* of the shooting squads, or Einsatzgruppen, have previously been referred to, and warrant close investigation. It is this data which even David Irving agrees is factual. (Although <u>that</u> is no proof of anything!)

This data is significant because mass shooting was the method by which every living soul was destroyed from hundreds of small Jewish villages in Eastern Europe; in them traditional and orthodox Jewish life ceased, leaving no trace.

Secondly, there were so many scattered killing sites that the Nazis found eleventh-hour exhumation was impossible. Many bodies remained in unmarked graves, to be discovered by farmers, or by grave robbers searching for gold teeth. The method of death was obvious, a bullet to the nape of the neck. There can be no deceptive talk of accidental death from epidemics and starvation when one of these mass graves is unearthed.

Thirdly, this was the method by which many hundreds of local civilians Lithuanians, Estonians, Latvians, Poles and Ukrainians, were turned into murderers, recruited to be murderers of their fellow countrymen, perhaps even of their neighbours, customers, employees, tradesmen and friends.

Plate 3. Memorial of the Destroyed Communities, Yad Vashem
Photo: Deslee Campbell, 2006.

These shooting squads were formed to eliminate opposition to the Reich in conquered territory, first in Austria, in 1938 then in occupied Czechoslovakia and Poland in 1939 and finally in the Baltic states and the Soviet Union in 1941. Following the victorious invading Reich Army across Eastern Europe these Special Operations Groups were ordered, in "Operation Barbarossa", to shoot communists, intellectuals, gypsies, "*People's Commissars, Jews in Party and State employment and other radical elements (saboteurs, propagandists, snipers, assassins, inciters)*"[17], partisans and their sympathisers. In a top-secret order of June 6, 1941 they were told: "I*t is a mistake to show mercy or respect for international law towards such elements..... when they are picked up in battle or resistance, they are, as a matter of principle, to be finished off immediately with a weapon*".[18] Thousands of Jews, especially religious, intellectual, and political leaders were shot by these squads and they herded Jews into ghetto cities such as Warsaw and Lublin. In this way many thousands of Jews who had recently fled eastwards, towards Russia, but who did not flee far enough, were caught anew in the German dragnet.

Plate 4. "Memorial Column for Jewish Heroes" by Buki Schwartz
Yad Vashem, Jerusalem. Photo: Deslee Campbell, 1990.

In occupied Russia the shooting squads were formed into four groups: A,B,C & D. Group A operated to the north towards Leningrad. Group B operated from Warsaw towards Moscow, Group C engaged in killing Aktionen from Brest Litovsk towards Karkhov, while group D swept south east from Lvov to Rostov. Whole communities were destroyed in the most thorough, ruthless and cold blooded manner.

They encouraged local pogroms which secret German documents refer to as "Self-cleansing".[19] They recruited willing locals, whose orders came from SS Officers, assisted by the Gestapo and German Police. Whole districts were systematically cleared. Victims were generally required to prepare their own mass gravesites in forested areas and stand beside them awaiting execution. Pistols, machine guns and also gas vans were used. Detailed, though incomplete reports exist: 195 reports are extant.

The shooting squads had to provide reports and tallies of their victims: numbers of males and females; Jews and Communists; with area totals and monthly totals. This provides some of the most damming material of the Shoah. Although we lack the complete set of reports, those we possess are extremely thorough. From them it is estimated that 1½ million East European Jews were shot and buried in mass graves. Some of the reports contain vivid descriptions of the most barbaric deeds.

Chapter 7
Railway Timetables are Important

Railway timetables, seemingly so inconsequential, have been proven by American Jewish historian, Raoul Hilberg, as providing vital proofs of Nazi genocidal activities as well as very good estimates of the numbers transported to the various death camps and concentration camps. Bureaucracies simply do not trundle empty trains from country to country for no reason, yet trains from Italy, Southern Greece, France, Belgium and other distant parts of Europe rolled continually into and away from Poland, epicentre of the Shoah, crossing many national borders and taking weeks to reach the main destinations, such as Auschwicz.

Plate 5. This cattle truck found in Poland

was sent to Yad Vashem in 1989. It was thoroughly clean
Photo: Deslee Campbell, 1990.

Each and every carriage, or more correctly van or cattle truck, for every train, had to be organised, delivered, scheduled, repaired and cleaned. Cleaned - leaving no trace of death, birth, miscarriage, suicide, disease and almost every experience of humanity in extremis. Each engine had to fuelled and watered, driven and timetabled, shunted and returned. Thousands of people were involved in this operation. The documentation has survived. It is this meticulously kept and amazingly preserved documentation of train movements and train capacities which has enabled the most accurate estimate of the number of Shoah victims to be made.

Plate 6. Memorial of the Deportees, Yad Vashem.
Photo: Deslee Campbell, 2009.

Each leg of each journey had to be paid for in the appropriate currency of the country of transit. The bitter irony is that national and Reich railways made a profit out of their trade in human flesh; as Jews who could afford to pay were sold a one way third class ticket. Payment for poor Jews had to be raised from abroad: American Jews making generous donations to help with the 'resettlement' of their kinsfolk. Thousands of trains made the long journey across Europe to Poland, and returned empty. Where, we may well ask the Holocaust deniers, were their multitudes of passengers when the camps were finally liberated?

Here is one example: On 20/12/'43, train number Da 101 carried Jewish passengers from Theresienstadt to Auschwitz. The next day it departed from Auschwitz and returned to Theresienstadt, totally empty. Two days later again it left on a further journey, taking more Jewish passengers to Auschwitz and returning empty. After Christmas, on 26th December, train number Da 101 took a third consignment of Jewish passengers to Auschwitz, returning empty on 27th. Here, in bureaucratic paperwork, we see the first step in a massive liquidation of the concentration camp of Theresienstadt, the so called `model ghetto', the camp whose operations so impressed visiting dignitaries from the International Red Cross; and about which Hitler made a propaganda film *"The Fuhrer Presents the Jews With a City"*.

Detailed confidential reports were provided to SS officials about each transport; with recommendations to improve efficiency of future operations. These reports included the number of cars, persons, destinations, stops, departure times and other mundane matters.

Here is one example of such a report, provided by one Captain Salitter written on 26th December about a five day rail-journey which transported 1007 Jews from Dusseldorf in Germany, to Riga in Latvia, between 12th December and 17th December, 1941: *"The food we (the guards) were served was sufficient and wholesome;"* he reported. *"Our two spotlights were extremely useful, and they will be necessary for future transports as well. Without adequate light, the guards would have been handicapped and hampered in the use of fire arms when needed"* and also *"I must mention favourably the support of the Red Cross, especially serving refreshments to the escort commando and giving them every possible assistance at the stations."*..... But let us remember that no one fed the passengers!

There are memoranda and invoices ordering trains from other European governments, and correspondence about disputes when the Reich Government failed to pay for the trains. These invoices are detailed: such as the one to the commander of Sobibor, invoice No.500, for 5 rail cars, raw weight: 25,000 kg. When one remembers that each cattle truck was packed beyond capacity, with from 60 to 100 people squashed into each, such a single invoice accounts for between 300 and 500 people.

Most of this rail-transport documentation was over-looked by the Nazis as they faced their defeat. Perhaps they considered it too inconsequential to be worth destroying. Most of it remained in the filing cabinets at the collapse of the Thousand Year Reich: rich evidence for true research.

Chapter 8
Camps

One well circulated leaflet, published by the Institute for Historical Review, asks "*Did Simon Wiesenthal* (the famous 'Nazi hunter') *once state in writing that 'there were no extermination camps on German soil?"* and then the pamphlet states: "*Yes. In Books and Bookmen, April, 1975 issue. He claims the "gassings" of Jews took place in Poland."*

This is actually not so much a question of geography as one of semantics. What were 'extermination camps' and who has established the definition?

Jewish Holocaust experts generally agree with a very limited definition: that there were only six 'death camps'. These were: Chelmno (1941), Belzec (1942), Sobibor (1942), Treblinka (1942), Majdanek, and Birkenau (Auschwitz II). All six were specifically established for the sole or primary purpose of mass extermination and all were in Poland.

Ground Plan of Auschwitz I

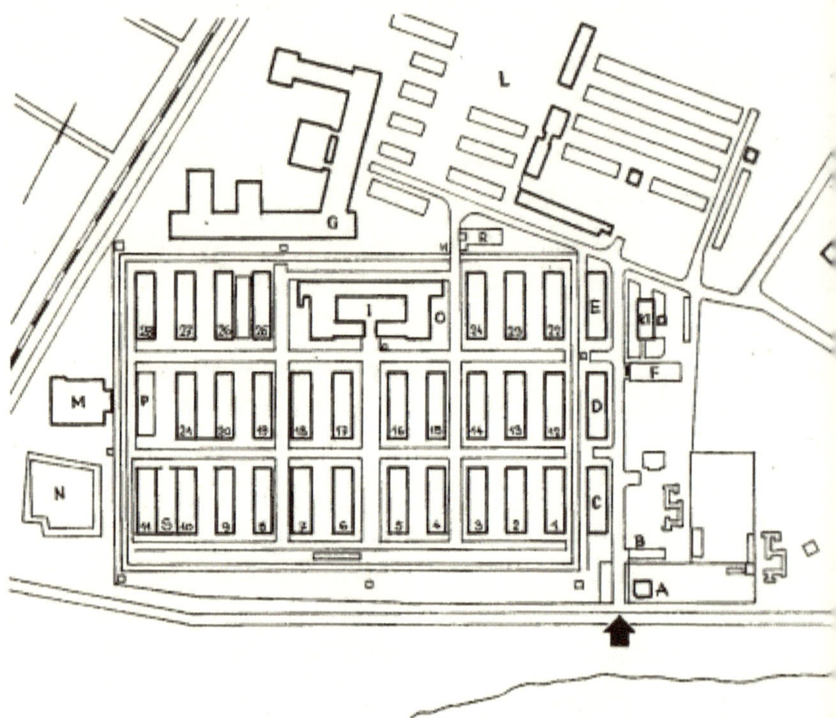

A Commandant's house	KI	Gas Chamber and crematorium
B Security Gate	L	Maintenance workshops
C Commandant's Office	M	Warehouse for possessions
D Admin Office	N	Execution place
E SS Hospital	O	Place for orchestra
F Political Dept. Offices	P	Laundry for SS
G Reception building	R	Security for section manager
H Entrance Gate	S	Execution wall
I Kitchen	1–28	Areas for prisoners

Auschwitz is somewhat different from the other five, as there were three Auschwitz complexes, hence the possibility for confusion, **and for**

disinformation. Only Auschwitz III was a slave-workers camp, although Holocaust deniers claim that rubber factory work was the true purpose of Auschwitz. In fact Birkenau (Auschwitz II) was mainly set up for extermination, and had four crematoria, one of which was accidentally damaged by American bombing raids on the rubber factory where the slave-labourers worked, and one of which was damaged by saboteurs. Auschwitz I had one crematorium.

Of course deliberate killings, even mass killings, also took place in other camps, generally called concentration camps, places such as Sachsenhausen (1936), Buchenwald (1937), Flossenburg (1938), Mauthausen (1938) Ravensbruck (1939), and Bergen-Belsen. These were in Germany and Austria. In Mauthausen, for example, 122,000 prisoners died. The heroine Violet Zabo, made famous by the book *"Carve her Name with Pride"*, was executed in Ravensbruck.

Mass killings also took place in deserted locations in the open air, such as the infamous valley of slaughter, Ponar; the Ninth Fort near Kovno; and in the ravines of Babi-Yar, on the outskirts of Kiev.

Nazi prisons, such as the Small Fort of Thresienstadt, were places of death: by disease, starvation, brutal torture and execution. Such killings also took place in Auschwitz I: its execution wall is a well known shrine.

Plate 7. Execution Wall, Auschwitz I.
Photo: David Campbell, 1992.

Hundreds of holding camps, such as Drancy in France and Westerbork in Holland, to which Anne Frank's family was first taken, did not usually include killing Aktionen, although, in them, some prisoners were tortured to death or executed by hanging or firing squad, and group hangings as reprisals for German deaths took place.

Jews were interred in ghettos as well as in concentration camps. In many respects life in these places was similar. Ghettos were generally within larger towns or cities. Suburbs were modified for the purpose, whereas, in general, camps were built from scratch for their specific purposes in more remote places. One exception to this is the small walled town of Theresienstadt, in Czechoslovakia, which was a sealed ghetto but is generally regarded as a concentration camp. This example proves that definitions are difficult: but of the 139,654 people interred in that town, only 17,320 survived.

Between 1942 and 1945 no new concentration camps were built and, as there was a severe labour shortage in Germany, there was more emphasis on forced labour in war related industries (but only the able-bodied were spared). For example prisoners in Dora-Mittelbau made V-2 rockets.

Twenty two of the largest killing sites are commemorated in the Hall of Remembrance, where the Eternal Flame burns at Yad Vashem in Jerusalem: Theresienstadt, Dachau, Stutthof, Lvov, Jasenovac, Klooga, Sobibor, Treblika, Auschwitz, Babi-Yar, Chelmno, Belzec, Bergen-Belsen, Ponar and many more.

The very first killing, however, was done in vans and ambulances which were driven around until the carbon monoxide exhaust accomplished its purpose. The euthanasia of Germany's intellectually disabled and mentally ill, more than 70,000 victims in all, was accomplished in this way.

This program was discontinued because of public outrage, and church opposition.

The technical experts from the program were simply ordered to relocate to the old castle at Chelmno (where 5,000 gypsies and 250,000 Jews were destined to die). These experts were later employed at Belzec, Treblinka and Sobibor: but the opponents were silent when it was Jews who were being killed.

Chapter 9
Documents and Reports

The archives of Yad Vashem contain over two million relevant documents from the period, from Allies, Axis powers and neutrals, from victims and perpetrators, and 50 million personal articles and memorabilia, as well as 30,000 eye-witness accounts.

Jewish Bureaucratic Documents

After 1939, once the Germans had ordered the formation of Jewish Councils, or Judenrat, to control every aspect of daily life in the ghettos, purely Jewish bureaucracies, with attendant paperwork, were created. The Jewish Councils had to report detailed statistics to the Reich for the allocation of rations, and, to tell the truth, their sole official purpose was the implementation of Reich policy, although they tried to maintain ghetto morale and to help their people. Adam Czerniakow, head of the Warsaw Judenrat, is greatly honoured because he suicided rather than assist the Nazis in selections for deportation (23/7/'42).

A few collections of these bureaucratic documents survived the liquidation of the ghettoes: from Lodz, Bialystok, Warsaw and Amsterdam. They contain details of the minute details of daily life and death. We know, for example, how many males and females died in each month of 1941 in the Lodz ghetto. We know that in one month 1,342 males and 792 females starved to death and 15 people froze to death. Only 13 females died of gunshot wounds while trying to escape or smuggle food, compared with 27 males. We know that the food ration was one and a half pounds of bread per week, and so the data goes on and on...

German Documents
1) Policy Documents

The extent and enormity of the Holocaust demanded that an overall policy to the Jewish people was in operation. While much of this policy was formulated in secret face-to-face meetings between Hitler and his inner circle, it had to be committed to writing as it filtered down the ranks of the bureaucracy and the SS. It must be assumed that orders given by the inner circle came from the very top, especially when men such as Himmler and Heydrich actually stated that the were passing on the Fuhrer's Orders. They would not have dared to lie about such matters: other high officials had been purged....

Broad policy statements are found in Hitler's speeches and writings, including in *"Mein Kamph"* (My Struggle) which Hitler wrote as early as 1925. In the Wannsee Conference, the `final solution' became open and official policy. From the distributed minutes of this Conference we learn that there was an overall plan for **all** of Europe's Jews, from as far afield as Ireland, Portugal and Turkey and that their numbers were known, their fate was on the drawing board.

2) Planning Documents

These include statements about the planned deportations of all Jews to `the east', planning for the activities of the Einsatzgruppen shooting squads, planning for the construction and operation of the death camps, and plans for their layout.

3) Written Instructions

One of the largest bodies of written material is composed of bureaucratic instructions, orders, telegrams and memoranda. The most damning of these were classified by the Nazis as `highly confidential'. The Nazis knew which of their deeds to keep to themselves. The handling and mass movement of millions of people from one end of Europe to the other would have been impossible without implementation instructions about the most mundane matters. One example was the written instruction of July '41, to Heydrich, which gave him the responsibility for *"making all necessary preparations...for an overall plan.. for the execution of the intended final solution of the Jewish question."*

Reports

1) Reports Provided for Hitler.

The Shooting Squads provided written reports that went direct to Hitler. For example on 1/8/'41 Gestapo Chief Muller sent a coded message: "*the Fuhrer is to be kept informed continually from here about the work of the Einsatzgruppen in the East including visual material of special interest such as photographs*".

Himmler reported to Hitler on 20/12/42 the exact number of Jews shot in Poland and U.S.S.R. for each month from August to November 1942... August = 31,246; September = 165,282; October = 95,735; November = 70,948.[20]

2) Implementation Reports

Some of the most damning material is in the form of reports provided to Reich officials by those in charge of the transports and the shooting squads. Detailed reports of the progress and problems of each transport was provided.

The shooting squads had to provide reports and tallies of their victims: how many males and females, Jews and communists, with area totals and monthly totals. These are readily available, along with vivid descriptions of the most barbaric deeds. These reports indict both the German instigators and the Baltic and Ukrainian civilians who carried out the killing `Actions'.

Here is an excerpt from a report of 31/7/'42 about the actions of Shooting Squads in Byelorussia (White Russia): "*..the treatment of Jewry in Byelorussia is a matter of political importance.... we have liquidated about 55,000 Jews in the past 10 weeks. In the area of Minsk county Jewry has been completely eliminated without any danger to manpower requirements*".[21]

Similarly one Karl Jager, SS Standartenfuhrer in Kovno dispatched a secret document with full tabulation on 1/12/'41 to the Commander of the Security Police: "*I can confirm today that Einsatzkommando 3 has achieved the goal of solving the Jewish problem in Lithuania. There are no more Jews in Lithuania, apart from working Jews and their families (about 34,500)*".[22]

Although these we lack the complete set of these reports, those we have are thorough. From their data it is estimated that over 1.4 million East European Jews were shot by pistols or machine guns and buried in widely scattered mass graves.[23]

Eye-Witness Reports

In some areas citizens compiled denunciations or protocols of crimes committed against Jewish citizens of their region. One such report, compiled on 5th July 1943, by three eminent doctors and four others from Kislovodsk and Leningrad, listed the Jewish medical personnel who had been killed, and named the nine children from one institution who were shot. "*The citizen Fingerut, who escaped the shooting of the Jews, gave detailed evidence*".[24] The protocol denounced and named the military Commander, the head of the Gestapo, and his assistant, for slaughtering 2000 Jews on 9/9/'42; including old people, women and children. It also lists seven documents in support of the denunciation including three official German documents, and evidence from Fingerut and eight other witnesses.

Chapter 10
Invoices

Without doubt the invoices and receipts connected with the acquisition of Zyclon B, which was used at Auschwitz and Majdanek, are the most significant commercial documents of this kind to have survived the war. Producers of the chemical were Dessauer Works for Sugar and Chemical Industry and distributed by the German Corporation for Combating Vermin (DEGESCHE) whose managing director was Dr. Gerhard Peters. Accounts to DEGESCHE for 1943 and 1944 totalled about 17 million Reichmarks.

A request of 5th April,'44, to Dr Peters, for a supply of 12,000 pounds of this brand of hydrogen cyanide pellets *"urgently needed by the Armed SS" exits.*[25] This is enough of the poison to provide a lethal dose for 84,000,000 million people.

A similar letter to Dr Peters (of 24th May,'44) reads: "*I would like to know how you view the durability of the special deliveries made to Oranienburg and Auschwitz. In case there are doubts about the duration of storage, we would have to use up the earlier shipments for disinfection and keep only fresh deliveries. Up to now there has not been any need to use anything. On the other hand, major quantities - that is actually the whole of the stored quantity may under certain circumstances be needed all at once*".[26] The writing of this letter coincided with the arrival of the first transports of Hungarian Jews.

Some who worked for this company were tried in 1946 by a British Military Tribunal.

Chapter 11
Relics and Remains

While thousands of abandoned spectacles and piles of shoes and clothing may not prove the deaths of their owners, huge piles of hair, from both women and little girls, and hundreds of sets of false teeth and artificial limbs are strongly incriminating of inhumanity, if not gross cruelty or murder. But it is the suitcases, marked with the names and addresses of their missing owners which most eloquently ask 'where now are the ones so named, and when will they return to claim their property?' Fifty years later the world is still waiting.

It is often the personal memorabilia; the baptismal certificates by which the children were 'Aryanised'; the faded yellow stars, their sewing threads still clinging to their edges; and the torn and threadbare camp uniforms; which often bring the Shoah from the realm of theory and endow it with the essence of humanity. Seeing them, we realise that Hitler's obedient servants did not kill six million people; they killed one individual person, six million different times.

Memorabilia, treasured relics, are concrete items from the past, which prevent memories from slipping into the shadowy world of dreams; though they have often belonged to the realm of nightmares. As time passes relics are being surrendered to the museums and archives for safekeeping and preservation.

Here is a partial list of items collected from Jews in the strongly Jewish area of Galicia, Poland up to 30th June, 1943, from a secret SS report by Katzmann, SS and Police Commander of Galicia: 20,952 gold wedding rings; 20,889 kg of gold rings with stones; 22,740 pearls; 11,730 gold teeth-bridges; 97,581 gold coins. Even fountain pens and propelling pencils were recorded - 7.495 kg of them: plus 7 complete stamp collections and 5 travel baskets of loose stamps. No record was made of the large quantity of furniture and textiles taken, but the report did give other details: of Jews who hid in subterranean bunkers, drain pipes, chimneys, sewerage pits, catacombs, attics, and inside furniture.[27]

While the remains from the various crematoria were generally disposed of by mixing the ash with earth or water, there still exists a quantity of about 7 tons of ash at Majdanek, which was one of the two death camps kept operational until the last possible minute. This pile of ash and bone fragments is estimated to be the last remains of 50,000 to 60,000 people.

Chapter 12
Film Material

Because modern filmmakers can make film material represent images in many creative, even false ways, we cannot always rely on photographic material, especially movie film, as evidence. It can and should be viewed to `flesh out' our understanding of what happened, and to support other documentation.

We must not ignore or discount them, however, but examine the photographs thoroughly, because human beings are very `visual learners'. In establishing our position on the issue of Holocaust denial, however, we must rely on the scientific and documentary evidence.

Historian Sybil Milton has written "millions of images taken by SS Propaganda teams and a smaller number of photographs taken by victims, bystanders and liberators have survived".[28]

A large number of photographs are held by Yad Vashem in Jerusalem, and by the Leo Baeck Institute in New York; while the museums attached to some concentration camps, like Auschwitz and Dachau, hold the originals of film with particular relevance to that camp.

Nazi's Photographs & Films

The Nazi perpetrators were, at first, not ashamed of what they were doing: in fact photographs were used as weapons of intimidation and persecution (e.g., of gentiles entering Jewish shops) and official photographs were part of routine official administrative records. As Germany's defeat became immanent, however, the Nazis tried to destroy the evidence of their ghastly deeds, but still hundreds of feet of movie film of many murders and of the inhuman conditions in the camps are extant.

Propaganda Films

Propaganda films on 'Jewish pestilence and criminality' were made in Lodz and Warsaw in 1940 and 1942, and screened to indoctrinate German soldiers, police and SS units. From these films, strong indications of Nazi genocidal intentions are clear.

Other movies, such as *"Jew Suss"* was publicly shown across occupied Europe, although Jews were forbidden to enter the theatres. They were designed to prove to the public that the Jews were dirty, diseased and dangerous.

Take for example these quotations from the film *"The Eternal Jew"*, made in November 1940: *"The Jew remains a root-less parasite, even when he is in power. While millions of native Germans were unemployed and in distress, Jews gained fantastic fortunes. Not by honest work but by usury, swindles and fraud."*

Not only did the Nazis make propaganda films against the Jews, they also made films for self-enhancement and self- aggrandisement. During the Hungarian deportations of 1944 they made a film showing the cruelty with which the Hungarian police drove young and old into the rail cars from the ghetto of Nagyvarad (home town of teenage diarist Eva Heyman). This film goes on to show the "tender" treatment received from German nurses by those who survived the journey to Kassa, when the SS took control of the convoy from the Hungarian guards.[29]

The Nazi's used films for propaganda, to demonstrate to selected audiences, such as the International Red Cross, that the Jews were well cared for in the ghettos. The prime example of the latter is the film made from 16th August to 11th September, 1944, in Theresienstadt, which was a fake model ghetto, with fake shops and fake schools. This camp was temporarily improved and normalised for the benefit of the film, but in reality it was simply a transit camp on the route to Auschwitz. Within three months, the Jews who had been forced to script, shoot and act in this film had been exterminated.

Liberator's Film Material

Allied soldiers who liberated the camps, including official war reporters and photographers, were shocked beyond belief by what they found. The British liberators of Bergen-Belsen reported that they could smell the stench from two miles away. They made a film of the liberation of this camp called *"Evidence For All Mankind."*

The Soviets made their own propaganda film: of their liberation of Auschwitz; and the Americans made a film *"Nazi Concentration Camps"*.

Hollywood Films

Hollywood style films can be extremely gripping, such as *"Schindler's List"*, and very accurate, like *"Escape From Sobibor"*, but they are primarily entertainment, not evidence. While they convey the feel and overall character of the Shoah, Hollywood films may contain factual errors.

Photographs

German Photographs

Official and unofficial German photographers took extensive still photographs. These include colour photographs such as those from the Lodz Ghetto, on display in the Sydney Jewish Museum.

There are 65 official photos of many aspects of daily life, work and punishment in Dachau, taken in 1933 and others in Dachau in 1938 as well as photos of the quelled Warsaw Ghetto Uprising, the most famous being of the little boy with hands raised. Amateurs and professionals photographed the burning synagogues on Kristallnacht (10/11/'38); the public burning of Jewish books in May 1933; even the mass shooting of naked men, women and children.

The data includes 250 photographs of medical experimentation and murder in Auschwitz and Janovska, which were submitted as evidence at the Nuremberg Trials of War Criminals 1947-1949.

Collections include *"The Warsaw Ghetto in Photographs: 206 Views made in 1941"*[30]; *"The Yellow Star"*[31]; *"The Warsaw Ghetto in Pictures: Illustrated Catalogue"*[32]; and an article by Sybil Milton in the Simon Wiesenthal Centre Annual 1 (1984) and *"An Illustrated Sourcebook of the Holocaust"* (3 vols.)[33]. A broader pictorial sourcebook for the Nazi era is Fredric Grunfeld's *"The Hitler File: A Social History of Germany and the Nazis, 1918-45."*[34]

The famous *"Auschwitz Album"*, consists of 185 still shots of Auschwitz and Birkenau, taken by one of the two official photographers on 26th May, 1944. The album was discovered five months later in an abandoned SS barracks at Dora Camp, 500 miles from Auschwitz, by survivor Lili Meier, who recognised members of her family and community in the album.[35]

The original owner had titled the album *"Resettlement of the Hungarian Jews"*. The Album was used in evidence at the 1961 Eichmann trial and the 1964 Frankfurt trials of 22 SS men, but it was published only in 1981. Photographs in the album *"A Day With the Camera in the Ghetto"* were taken in the Warsaw Ghetto, by an off-duty German soldier.

Of his photos of the Warsaw Ghetto, Joe Heydecker, a German serviceman, said "(the photos) *were taken that the shame should not be forgotten, to keep alive the shriek I wanted the world to hear"*. Heydecker's album is called *"Where is Thy Brother Abel?: Documentary Photographs of the Warsaw Ghetto"*.[36]

By contrast, the last commandant of Treblinka, Kurt Franz, assembled an album of his 'work' called *"The Best Years of My Life"* which, twenty years later, was confiscated by West German police.

Jewish Photographs

Mendel Grossman, a Jewish lab. technician who perished in Auschwitz took 10,000 photographs in the Lodz Ghetto, which he buried in tin cans in a hollow window-sill.

Members of the Jewish resistance took photographs of the Warsaw Ghetto uprising; and of women entering the Birkenau gas chambers in 1944, which were smuggled out of the camp.

Allied Photographs

Both personal and official photographs were taken on the day of liberation. This includes 38 photographs from Ohrduf, Buchenwald, Gardelegen and Nordhausen.

The British recorded Bergen-Belsen; the Soviets, Majdanek and Auschwitz; and the Americans Dachau and Mauthausen. Other photographs were recovered from retreating guards and SS men.

The revisionist claim that photographed camp inmates were healthy and well fed. In some instances newly arrived deportees may have been photographed, as a flood of deportees constantly arrived, even in the last days of the war. It was as though Hitler was determined to take as many Jewish lives as possible, before taking his own.

Certainly the photographs and reports of the Allied soldiers to whom fell the task of cleaning up the camps and tending the dying prove the astonishing suffering, starvation and mortality among camp inmates. So many of the subjects of these photographs are living skeletons, certainly thousands continued to die after the liberation, and many were too ill to leave the camps after liberation.

Chapter 13
Testimony

In recent decades verbal testimony has come under attack, as a source of evidence. This is understandable, as memories may have dulled the details and the facts after half a century. In the stress and haste of the actual events, the factual details may not have been memorised at the time: or misinformation supplied to them may have been accepted as fact.

Survivor's testimony, while being a very valid aspect of the whole picture, focuses on personal details, whereas modern scholarship focuses upon the broader picture. This is not to discount the personal memories, but to understand that they are not infallible, and form one of many facets of evidence. It is most important to understand the significant but subjective nature of survivor's testimony, because it can play into the hands of Holocaust deniers if an item in one testimony is mistaken.

Jan Karski's Testimony

Verbal reports were provided in person by the former Polish officer now known by his pseudonym, Jan Karski, about his secret July 1942 visits inside both the Warsaw ghetto and the Belzec death camp. Jan Karski took urgent messages from the Jewish leaders to the President of the Polish Republic in exile; to British Foreign Secretary, Anthony Eden, and to American President, Roosevelt. His own oral message was: *"unless the Allies take some unprecedented steps, regardless of the outcome of the war, the Jews will be totally exterminated"*. Such unprecedented steps suggested included dropping leaflets to inform the German people of the genocide, the bombing of railway lines, pre-publicised reprisal bombings on non-military targets, supply of arms to the Jewish resistance and hunger strikes by other Jews.

No action was taken to prevent the slaughter of Jews and Professor Jan Karski (Mr. Vitold) was so decimated by his experiences and the failure of his mission that he did not speak of it for thirty-six years.

After over three decades from the time he took his message from the ghetto to world leaders he was prepared to speak: "*It wasn't humanity, it was some ... hell. It was not a world. It was not a part of humanity. I was not part of it. I did not belong there. I never saw such things.. nobody wrote about this kind of reality. I never saw any theatre, I never saw any movie (like this).. this was not the world. I was told that these were human beings - they didn't look like human beings. I was sick. Even now I don't go back in my memory*".[37]

Liberator's Testimony

While Holocaust deniers may try to make what they call `the photographs' say anything they choose, they cannot make the living testimony of the Allies who liberated the camps say other than what those soldiers did say.

Liberators gave evidence in many of the trials and their testimony is that hundreds of the unburied dead were still in the camps at liberation, and that gas chambers <u>were</u> used to liquidate victims.

Bystander's Testimony

Many local East European residents were anti-Semitic themselves and therefore have no vested interest in exaggerating the Jew's suffering, yet their testimony agrees with that of the victims. For example: local Poles reported that three SS men arrived in Belzec in October,'41 and demanded a draft of twenty Polish workers. These workers constructed two barracks, and a gas chamber, according to a set of plans, before being dismissed on 23rd December, 1941.

On 5th September, 1945, a committee of leading citizens of Kharkov; priests, professors and city councillors; wrote a protocol of Nazi atrocities[38]: *"barbarity inflicted on innocent citizens was confirmed by evidence obtained from witnesses..... medical experts and from other reliable documents"* and *"within the area of the ghetto there was a so-called 'living grave' from which, after the killings, groans were heard from people who had been buried alive there"*.

Near Kharkov on 7/1/42 a woman, Anastasya Zakharovna Osmachko, her son Vladimir, and eleven village people were caught by German soldiers looking at a shooting site. They were machine-gunned, but the woman fainted and lay amongst the dead and dying all day, before escaping, and testifying.[39]

In Communist countries such information from locals has not been spoken about openly, but this is beginning to change. French film maker Claude Lanzman interviewed a cross section of such people for his nine hour long film *"Shoah"*.

German Testimony

Felix Kersten, in his Memoirs (written between 1940 and 1945) recorded that he was told by Himmler on November 11,'41 (i.e., before the Wannsee Conference): that *"the destruction of the Jews is being planned... Now the destruction of the Jews is imminent."*

Similarly, seven days later, a confidential briefing was given to the German press corps in which Rosenberg told them that the Jewish question could *"only be solved in a biological extermination of all Jews in Europe."*

In November, 1942, Johann Paul Kremer, an SS doctor in Auschwitz, wrote a detailed account of gassing arrangements, selection and preparation of victims, removal of gold teeth and hair. He recorded receiving secret orders upon his arrival at the camp on 30th October, 1942. Kremer's Diary was used in the successful prosecution of Faurisson on the charge of falsification of history.

Witness Testimony

The Yad Vashem archives record the life experiences of those who suffered during the Holocaust, yet survived. This witness material is provided freely by Jews from around the world. It is often from this material that the "Righteous From Among the Nations" (Righteous Gentiles) are identified, and subsequently honoured with a ceremony, a medal, or the planting of a tree. Apart from the 30,000 testimonies gathered by Yad Vashem, people and Jewish institutions throughout the world are publishing oral testimony.

The Hall of Names

The Hall of Names was established in 1968 as the depository of the "*Pages of Testimony*" in which the names of Shoah victims are recorded, in person or by mail. By 1990 three million names of those who perished had been recorded by surviving relatives and friends. This recording was one of the purposes for which this Martyrs and Heroes Remembrance Authority was established on the Mount of Remembrance:

"I will give to them in my house
and within my walls
a place and a name better than sons and daughters.
I will give them an everlasting name
that shall not be cut off."
Isaiah 56:5

Chapter 14
Issues of Death

It is difficult to focus on aspects of the atrocities committed. They are very important, but it is not these which separate the Shoah from other historic barbarities such as the Mongol invasion or the Burma Railway, but the totality of the overall plan. The Shoah was intended to be the total destruction of all Jews under Nazi control: even those of part German/part Jewish heritage; even those awarded with Iron Cross decorations in World War I; even those who had made world famous medical discoveries; even great scientists whose help Germany might need. Hitler openly refuted the notion of saving the "one good Jew".

Death Marches

Death marches had begun as early as 1943, when some ghettos were being liquidated. On 8th July, 1943, the Kovno ghetto inhabitants were forced to walk from Poland into Germany, after 2,000 of the 6,000 inmates were shot.

Three weeks later one of the Warsaw ghettos was liquidated with 3,600 people being marched the 130 km. to Kutno. One thousand were lost on the journey.

After the Battle for Stalingrad in late 1942, the fortunes of war on the Eastern Front turned. Soviet Forces advanced on the shrinking Third Reich, and, after D-Day, the British and Americans advanced on the second front.

Intensified efforts were made by the Nazis to (1) expand the rate of exterminations (2) dismantle the least efficient death camps (3) destroy as much evidence as possible (3) move the stronger camp inmates deep into the German heartland.

Death Marches were again instituted. Prisoners were therefore herded out of camps and forced to make protracted marches, sometimes at the run, through the snow, without food or water. Those who fell were shot, the roads into Germany being littered with their unburied bodies.

Of those who set out at the run, from Auschwitz on 17th January, 1945, Nobel Laureate, Elie Wiesel, then a boy of fifteen, was one of 15,000 to survived. His father was one of the 51,000 who died (while 48,000 men and 18,000 women remained in the camp and were liberated by the Soviets).

He recorded it graphically, poetically, in *"Night"*: "*Our limbs were numb with cold despite the running, our throats were parched, famished, breathless, on we went. We were masters of nature, masters of the world. We had forgotten every thing - death, fatigue, our natural needs. Stronger than cold or hunger, stronger than the shots and the desire to die, condemned and wandering, mere numbers, we were the only men on earth*."

Two other camps were evacuated eight days later, on 25th January. Of the 4,000 who were force-marched from Blechhammer Camp, 1,000 died en-route; and of the 50,000 who marched out of Stutthof over 50% perished on the death-march.

Later, in April 1945, Mauthausen was evacuated. First, over 7000 Buchenwald prisoners were killed, while another 28,250 were evacuated, just four days before the American liberators came.

The enormous death tolls from these forced route-marches suggest the horrors and sufferings inflicted upon sick and starving prisoners, who had already suffered so much.

War Crimes Trials

A main thrust of `revisionism' has been to claim that the Allies were guilty of crimes (in bombing Hiroshima, Cologne and Dresden) and therefore had no moral right to try the Nazis; that the Nuremberg Trials were `kangaroo courts'; and that torture was used to extract confessions.

Here again the very enormity of the data is over-looked. There are still war crimes trials continuing today: most of which do not rely at all on Nazi confessions.

Trials have been conducted by both military and civil courts; and these trials have occurred in many different nations, including Australia, Poland, Hungary, France, Britain, U.S.A., Canada, Israel and the Soviet Union. To attack the justice of the trials is to attack the legal systems of virtually every democratic country of the world, over a period of fifty years! Not only that, but democratic West Germany conducted War Crimes Trials of its own!

Fortunately there were survivors of **all** the death camps: it was not necessary to rely upon confessions, whether given freely or under torture. For example two prisoners escaped from Chelmno Death Camp in January 1942: Michael Podchlebnik and Jacob Grojanowski. Two more wounded slave-prisoners escaped the final liquidation of the Sonderkommando workers of Chelmno. These men, Mordekhai Zurawaski and Shimon Srebrnik, testified at the 1945 trial of Chelmno war criminals in Poland; and the Eichmann trial in Israel.

The dead were not left without a witness.

Apart from witness testimony, the accused did give witness at many war crimes trials. In his sworn testimony Hoss, commander of Auschwitz, said that Himmler had given him top secret orders to plan the installations at Auschwitz and that: *"the Jews are the sworn enemies of the German people and must be eradicated.... Eichmann decided to try and find a gas which was in ready supply and which would not entail special installations for its use, and to inform me when he had done so.... We calculated... it would be possible to kill about 800 people simultaneously with a suitable gas. These figures were borne out later in practice."*[40] He wrote similar material in his autobiography. Was he tortured into writing this tome?

The mass of testimony, given under strict legal conditions, and subject to the most thorough cross examination and scrutiny, must be some of the most thoroughly attested, and therefore reliable testimony ever given. Although such evidence is highly subjective, of its type it is robust evidence in both quantity and quality.

Estimates of Killing Capacity and Population Statistics

The pall of smoke that hung over the camps, the sickly smell of the burnings, and the sight of flames continually leaping into the air from tall chimneys indicated far and wide that cremation was in progress.

The capacity of the four crematoria at Auschwitz-Birkenau provides some idea of the numbers killed there. On 22/6/1982 Scheffler, who was involved in the events, told historian Gerald Fleming during an interview: *"From mid 1943 there were 46 combustion chambers in operation in the crematoria of the liquidation complex at Auschwitz"* (a capacity of 10,000 in 24 hours).

When demographic data is studied in detail it becomes obvious that there was a very dramatic fall in Jewish numbers between about 1939 and 1942 so that today there are, in the entire world, fewer Jews than the 16 million peak of 1939. While about 40,000 Jews per year were able to leave Europe between 1933 and 1938 this in no way compares with the 1948-50 figures of over 100,000 a year; nor the 1989-90 figures of over 150,000 a year. Many Jews fled from Germany, to the east and the west, but did not leave Europe. It was difficult to find nations of refuge, and to abandon possessions and family.

When the estimates of Jewish populations which were used at the Wannsee Conference are compared with the world population of Jews IN 1990: i.e., 4½ million in Israel, 6 million in the U.S.A., 2 million in the former Soviet Union it can be discerned that the dramatic drop occurred in Europe. In 1939, Europe had 9 million Jews. It now has fewer than 2½ million. This drop can be compared with the sweep of the Black Plague across Europe.

Forensic Evidence

After the War, expert medical committees were established to open mass graves and establish the causes of death.[41] The findings and reports of these studies is, itself, an enormous study.

Other forensic study has been applied to documents, items said to be made from parts of the human body (such as hair) and items submitted as evidence in court.

Plate 7. Memorial to Zanosz Korczak who was gassed in Treblinka
with his two nearly hundred orphans.
Photo: Deslee Campbell, 1990.

Chapter 15
Other Evidence

There are many other categories of data upon which the traditionalist's and expert's case for the Shoah rests.

Works of Art

The art museum of Yad Vashem contains many moving drawings and paintings created in ghettoes, in hiding places, and in the camps, often executed on torn fragments of paper. Of particular importance is the very substantial collection of children's art from Theresienstadt. Most of this depicts happy subjects, because the children were not encouraged to dwell on their sufferings, but sometimes the harsh truths were illustrated.

Adult artists, on the other hand, who saw what no camera saw, sketched most vividly and at immense personal risk, the horror of their surroundings and the faces of their tortured and starving companions. Some of this work has survived.

Three dimensional religious objects such as candle holders, and Hanukkah lights were ingeniously made from whatever materials were at hand, to keep the flame of the spirit alive, and to rekindle faith. Useful items and small decorative pieces were also painstakingly created. At immense personal risk, artists and writers strove to express their souls, to symbolise their emotions in their art. By this the human spirit triumphed.

The Holocaust museums also house post-Shoah sculptural and two dimensional works, by which survivors have continued to express their responses to their experiences. Immediately upon her release from Auschwitz and a Death March to Hamburg, seventeen year old Ella Lieberman immersed her energies into sketching these memories, as a therapeutic outlet which assisted her to take up the strands of a normal life once again. Similarly the work of renowned sculptor Elsa Pollak, whose work can be found at Yad Vashem, and at the Sydney Jewish Museum, draws its inner meaning from her Auschwitz experience.

Literary Works

These include letters, poems, prayers, and religious writings which tell us about how the writers felt as much as what was happening to them. There were Literary Circles in the better organised ghettos, and poetry was written by children as well as by adults. Such angst-filled expressions are only written by those who know to fear the very worst. What do children have with such things when life is good and there is nothing to fear.

THE BUTTERFLY

The last, the very last,
So richly, brightly, dazzlingly yellow.
Perhaps if the sun's tears would sing
against a white stone...
Such, such a yellow
Is carried lightly way up high.
It went away I'm sure because it wished to
kiss the world goodbye.
For seven weeks I've lived here,
Penned up inside this ghetto
But I have found my people here.
The dandelions call to me
And the white chestnut candles in the court.
Only I never saw another butterfly.
That butterfly was the last one.
Butterflies don't live in here,

In the ghetto.
Written in Theresienstadt 4/6/1942
by Pavel Friedmann aged 12 years

© Yad La Yeled
   Beit Lohamei Hagetaot
   Naharia, Israel.

Victim's Diaries

Many hundreds of diaries were written in ghettos, only some have survived. Some were written by ordinary people, men, women and children. The writings of Kitty Hart, Anne Frank and Eva Heyman and of boys like David Rubinowicz and Yitskhok Rudashevski have become fairly popular literary works, but many diaries remain unpublished, or are available only in the original languages: Hungarian or Yiddish perhaps.

Of particular importance for study are collections of diary type material: official daily records of ghetto life; Emmanuel Ringelblum's *"Oneg Shabbat"*[42] and Chaim Kaplan's *"Scroll of Agony - Warsaw Ghetto Diary"*[43] are very significant for their size and content. The former contains an archive of documents, diaries, newspapers and literary works of the Warsaw Underground, painstakingly collected, and saved.

On the other hand, some diary material was written in the camps: such as the *"Auschwitz Scrolls"*, written by prisoners, Sonderkommandos, doing slave labour within sight of the crematoria[44]. *"Letters From No-where"* [45], testaments written by the slave-labourers in Chelmno, in April, 1943, was handed to a Polish peasant who gave it to Soviet officials after the war. These letters constitute some of the most terrifying diary material ever to have been written.

Eye-witnesses Diaries

Some sympathetic gentiles wrote diary entries about what they saw and knew.

Here is what a Lithuanian Woman Doctor wrote in her diary: "*15/10/'41.... Thousands of people humiliated, without any protection, worse than animals, and all because they have 'other blood.'*"

"*30/10/41 ... Again (on 28th October) 10,000 people have been taken out of the ghetto to die. They selected old people, mothers with their children, those not capable of working...at the Ninth Fort prisoners had been digging deep ditches, and when the people were taken there, it was already clear to everybody that this was death. They broke out crying, wailed and screamed. Some tried to escape...*"[46]

Chapter 16
Why Did it Happen?

This is far too large a topic to be covered in one chapter but here are some sign-posts.

1. Hitler was probably motivated by megalomania and/or hatred.
2. Hitler used parliamentary institutions to achieve power. He was legitimate.
3. Hitler appealed to the German 'hip pocket nerve' in three ways: he stirred up the people against the victors of World War I and their demand for war reparations, he accused Jews of being money-hungry and keeping Germans poor and he promised economic prosperity under his own leadership.
4. Hitler kept his plans secret and told lies so that few really knew what was happening until it was too late.
5. Hitler appealed to latent ideas of racial superiority and xenophobia.
6. He appealed to exaggerated national pride.
7. He used powerful and modern propaganda techniques.
8. He used pseudo-science that seemed trustworthy, and impressed ordinary folk.
9. The churches were sidelined as both Catholic and Lutheran churches were imbued with anti-Semitism. Catholicism inherited this from the 4th century church fathers such as John Chrysostom, Ambrose of Milan, St Jerome and Augustine of Hippo. Protestants inherited it from both John Calvin and Martin Luther.[47]
10. The Catholic Church was neutralised early, by a mutual agreement to stay out of each other's business.
11. Hitler's was a death-cult and involved a potent mixture of

German pre-Christian religion, witchcraft, the occult, Roman militarism, 'emperor'-worship and pagan religion.

Chapter 17
Epilogue

It behoves every intelligent and mature person, religious **or** secular, to consciously try to educate themselves about the Holocaust: to gain a little more understanding this year, than was gained last year. This is not an issue that should be regarded as touching Jews, rather than gentiles, nor which touches religious gentiles, rather than the non-religious. This is everyone's history, everyone's business and it could happen again: remember Pol Pot in Cambodia and Idi Amin in Uganda.

If we ignore the Holocaust, or shrink from confronting it, or if we are hoodwinked by Hitler's duplicity, or harbour sneaking doubts that perhaps, just perhaps, the deniers are right, or if we abandon the Jewish people to carry the memories, the knowledge, and the responsibility for educating the general public alone, then, in our generation, we nullify the victory that our forebears succeeded in denying Hitler. We posthumously grant him an immoral victory.

Appendix 1

Who Were They?

Adolf Hitler: Fuhrer of the Third Reich

Rudolf Hess: Hitler's Deputy

Adolf Eichmann: SS Obersturmbannfuhrer Gestapo Head of Jewish Affairs

Heinrich Himmler: Reichsfuhrer SS. Chief of Police & Minister of Interior

Reinhard Heydrich: SS Obergruppenfuhrer. Head of Reich Security Main Office

Martin Bormann: Hitler's personal secretary

Dr Rudolf Lange: Strumbannfuhrer; Commander of Security Police & SD in Latvia

Dr Freisler: Secretary of State, Reich Ministry of Justice

Dr Alfred Meyer: SA Obergruppenfuhrer; State Secretary in the Reich Ministry for the Occupied Eastern Territories

Dr Wilhelm Stuckart: State Secretary in the Reich Ministry of the Interior

Erich Neumann: Secretary of State & deputy of the Plenipotentiary for the Four Year Plan

Dr Joseph Buhler: Secretary of State in one part of Poland

Dr Martin Luther: Undersecretary of State in the Reich Ministry of Foreign Affairs

Heinrich Muller: SS Gruppenfuhrer. Chief of Gestapo in the Reich Security Main Office

Josef Goebbels: Gauleiter of Berlin & Reich Minister of Propaganda

Odilo Globocnik: SS Gruppenfuhrer, commander of the SS in Lublin & Triest. Commander/Operation Reinhard

[1]. Trial of the Major War Criminals before the International Military Tribunal, Nuremberg 14/11/1945-1/10/1946 VI, Nuremberg, 1947 pp 214-216 reprinted in "Documents of the Holocaust: Selected Sources on the Destruction of the Jews of Germany, Austria, Poland and the Soviet Union." [Hereafter referred to as "Documents of Yad Vashem"]

Editors: Y.Arad, Y.Gutman, A. Margaliot. Published by Yad Vashem and Pergamon, 1981. p. 360.

[2]. Gerald Fleming, "Hitler & the Final Solution" Pages 101-107

[3]. Gill Seidel "The Holocaust Denial" from

"Beyond the Pale Collective" (Leeds, 1986).

[4]. Yehudit Kleinman Ed. "Letters From Nowhere - Letters from the Nazi-occupied Countries" (in Hebrew) (Yad Vashem Publishing House, Jerusalem, 1988).

[5]. Original typed list in "Documents of Yad Vashem" Page 255

in German, with English translation pages 253-4

[6]. Protocol of Wannsee Conference Page 249

Documents of Yad Vashem

[7]. A German report on this matter sent to the Order Police in District Lublin on 15/10/43 is held in the Archives of the Polish Interior Ministry in: Jewish Historical Institute Warsaw.

[8]. "Documents of Yad Vashem" page 108.

[9]. "Documents Yad Vashem", page 247.

[10]. "Documents of Yad Vashem".

[11]. "Documents of Yad Vashem", page 444..

[12]. "Documents of Yad Vashem", page 342.

[13]. "Documents of Yad Vashem", page 274.

[14]. "Documents of Yad Vashem", pages 350-352.

[15]. "Documents of Yad Vashem", page 351.

[16]. see H.Trevor-Roper, "Hitler's Secret Conversations"

(New York: Signet, 1961).

[17]. Extract from guidelines by Heydrich for Higher SS and Police Leader in the Occupied Soviet Union, July 2, 1941. Yad Vashem Archives 0-4/53-1.

[18]. Extract From the Commissar's Order for "Operation Barbarossa," June 6, 1941. "Documents of Yad Vashem", page 377.

[19]. "Einsatzgruppe A: General Report up to October 15, 1941" in "Documents of Yad Vashem", page 389.

[20]. R. Hilberg "The Destruction of European Jews"

(Chicago, 1967), page 256

[21]. Secret Report from Kube: Generalkommissar for Byelorussia to Reichkommissar for Ostland Heinrich Lohse.

Minsk, 31/7/1942. "Documents of Yad Vashem", pages 411-413.

[22]. "Documents of Yad Vashem", pages 398-400.

Original is in the Yad Vashem Archives.

[23]. R. Hilberg cited above page 256.

[24]. Evidence of Witnesses on the Deportation and Killing of the Jews of Kislovodsk from "Documents Accuse" II Moscow, 1945. pp 140-42. "Documents of Yad Vashem" pages 427-430.

[25]. Nuremberg document N1-9909

[26]. Nuremberg document NI-9908

[27]. Final Report by Katzmann, Commander of the SS & Police

in the District of Galicia, on "the Solution of the Jewish Problem" in Galicia

Reich Secret Document To Higher SS & Police Leader East

SS Obergruppenfuhrer & General of the Police Kruger.

"Documents of Yad Vashem", pages 335-341.

[28]. "Images of the Holocaust" in "Holocaust & Genocide Studies Vol. 1, No. 1, page 27 (1986).

[29]. From "The Auschwitz Album " page 20.

[30]. Photographs by Albert Cusian and Erhard Joseph Knobloch Ulrich Keller, ed. New York: Dover 1984.

[31]. Gerhard Schoenberner London 1969.

[32]. YIVO New York 1970.

[33]. Zose Szajkowski, New York, 1977.

[34]. New York, 1979.

[35]. "The Auschwitz Album" Lili Meier. Text by Peter Hellman. Radom House New York.

[36]. trans. George Vigar Sao Paulo, Brazil (1981).

[37]. Oral testimony from the Claude Lansman film "Shoah".

[38]. "Documents of Yad Vashem", pages 421ff.

[39]. "Documents of Yad Vashem", page 424.

[40]. "Documents of Yad Vashem", pages 350-352..

[41]. "Documents of Yad Vashem", page 424.

[42]. E.Ringleblum "Archives of the Jewish Underground." October 1939 to about August 1942.

[43]. C.A.Kaplan."Scroll of Agony - Warsaw Ghetto Diary" Sept.1, 1939 - Aug.4, 1942. Tel Aviv, 1966.

[44]. See Ber Mark "The Scrolls of Auschwitz" (Tel Aviv, 1985).

[45]."Letters From Nowhere - the Letters of Jews from the Nazi-occupied Counties" written in Yiddish & Polish. Published in Hebrew By Yad Vashem Jerusalem, 1988.

[46]. Y. Kutorgene "Kovno Diary" 1941-42.

see Documents of Yad Vashem pages 405-6.

[47] See the Youtube video *Let the Lion Roar* by Derrek Frank.

Don't miss out!

Visit the website below and you can sign up to receive emails whenever Deslee Campbell publishes a new book. There's no charge and no obligation.

https://books2read.com/r/B-A-LSULB-PSQAF

BOOKS 2 READ

Connecting independent readers to independent writers.

Also by Deslee Campbell

Memorable Christians
Phoebe's Sister's: Women Leaders in Early Christianity
Phoebe's Sisters: Women Leaders in Early Christianity
Phoebe's Sisters : Women Leaders in Early Christianity
Bright Shining Lights of an Earlier Era
Shining Lights of the Reformation
Shining Lights of the Reformation
Remarkable Post-Reformation Christians
Remarkable Post-Reformation Christians
Remarkable Post-Reformation Christians
Modern Christian Martyrs
Modern Christian Martyrs
Modern Christian Martyrs
Modern Christian Martyrs ready.doc
Christian Women We Should Remember
Great Christian Men We Have Forgotten
Great Christian Men We Have Forgotten
Great Christian Men We Have Forgotten
Christian Women Leaders of the 20th Century

Shoah Series
Confronting Holocaust Denial

Standalone
The Topkapi Beggar
Voices From The Silence
Why a Roman Emperor Rebuilt Jerusalem and Jerash
Why a Roman Emperor Rebuilt Jerusalem and Jerash
Stones, Walls and Watchmen
Mothers in Israel
Ecclesia a Long Journey to Tomorrow
St Paul's Olive Tree Metaphor

Watch for more at www.synagogueandchurch.com.